COURBET

SANDRA PINTO

First American edition published by Grosset & Dunlap, Inc.
All rights reserved
Translated from the Italian by Diane Goldrei
Translation copyright © 1971 by Thames and Hudson, London
Copyright © 1969 by Sadea Editore, Firenze
Library of Congress Catalog Card Number: 74-122023

Printed and bound in Italy

Life and Works

Jean Désiré Gustave Courbet was born on 10 June 1819 in Ornans, a village in the Loue valley, not far from Besançon in Franche Comté, a region which was also the birthplace of Fourier, Proudhon and Hugo, all of whom were important to Courbet. His father, Eléonor Régis Courbet, a small but dedicated landowner, farmed his land at Flagey, about ten miles from Ornans. A deep feeling for the countryside, for village and peasant life, for the surrounding landscape – the craggy rocks of Ornans, the coniferous forests of Franche Comté, the picturesque banks of the Loue – was the underlying source of Courbet's vision. Family ties had an equally important effect on his art. Although he was the eldest son, his relationship with his mother was less important than that with his father who exerted a powerful influence on him. Of his four younger sisters, the closest to Courbet was Juliette, the youngest, and twelve years his junior. With the exception of Clarisse, who died in childhood, his other sisters – Zoé, who later married the painter Reverdy, and Zélie, who was to die before her brother, in 1875 – also posed frequently for Courbet. His family was thus the source of inspiration for his very real, hard-working and kindly women, to whose restrained sensuality Courbet gives a gamine and romantic quality, which did not offend provincial propriety. They are very different from the women the disillusioned Courbet was to paint in later years – the frankly seductive and untrustworthy worldly women of the cities.

As a country boy, Courbet learned more from nature and his free and simple way of life than from his studies at school, the purpose of which he could never fathom. At the age of twelve, he was given his first drawing lessons by Father Beau of the ' little' seminary in Ornans. At eighteen, he entered the Collège Royal in Besançon, and was allowed to attend, outside school hours, the free painting courses given by Charles Antoine Flajoulot, a follower of David. His days at the college were brightened by his friendship with his cousin Max Buchon, whose political beliefs he was to share, and whose *Essais poétiques* he illustrated with four lithographs. Apart from this friendship, his years in college were an oppressive experience, to be forgotten as soon as possible. In prison in 1871, Courbet confessed: 'When I have nightmares, they are nearly always memories of my school days.' As for his painting, when he arrived in Paris in 1840 he must have felt as though he was starting at the beginning again. Nevertheless, Flajoulot's teaching – a strict classicism, somewhere between that of David and Gros – proved to be a more than adequate basis for a promising career, judging by an early work like the *Portrait of Régis Courbet* (*pl. 1*). The work already contains the germ of Courbet's ' true allegory '. But for the light falling on the man's cheek and forehead and revealing his features, no other element is presented as instantaneous reality, instead, each element tends to have a permanent, archetypal quality: look, for example, at the cap with the slightly turned down peak, or the left arm resting on the arm of the chair, or the right hand slipped inside the waistcoat. Visual reality thus becomes the expression of the moral and social values which the painter wishes to convey to us: the honesty and simplicity of the man whom we know to have been passionately interested in technological and philanthropic experiments on the land.

After the death of Flajoulot in 1840, Courbet asked and was granted leave to go to Paris. The pretence of studying law was kept up for a few months, but neither Gustave nor his family really believed it. It was Courbet's father who arranged, through a Parisian acquaintance, for him to join the studio of the academic painter Steuben. But Courbet, now twenty-one years old, already knew, if only intuitively, what he wanted. He chose another teacher, the painter Hesse, whose school was more liberal. He went to museums and zealously copied the Venetian, Spanish, Dutch and Flemish masters of the sixteenth to the eighteenth centuries. In 1866, dictating some notes for an autobiography, he said that when he saw Delacroix's paintings he was able to formulate his aims: 'The only way is to go like lightning through these different approaches' in order to achieve 'from the very first, paintings which will equal the best works in our museums.' He instinctively grasped one important truth: with David a cycle in art history had come to a close; the generation of Delacroix, Gros and Géricault had taken the right steps, those towards freedom and energy. If these gains were to be conserved, a commitment was necessary. Just as Romanticism was about to take a Parnassian turn in the uncommitted slogan of art for art's sake, Courbet chose the slogan 'socialists of all sects'. All the excitement of these feverish discoveries is expressed in one of his first self-portraits, known as *Despair* (*pl. 2*), painted in the winter of 1840-41. We can be sure that his friend the painter François Bonvin, who was his guide during his first year in Paris, and who was to be one of his most devoted followers, must have taken him to Louis Philippe's Spanish Gallery. As Toussaint has observed, the work is a careful pastiche of Zurbarán, by whom there were at least eighty-two paintings in the gallery. The colour, the triumph of light over shadow, is Spanish in origin. The work also recalls Delacroix's theatrical imagination, and, above all, Géricault's obsessive study of faces.

In 1841, Courbet went to Le Havre with his friend Urbain Cuenot. In this period of extreme emotional susceptibility, the journey became an important experience, as he wrote in a letter to his parents: 'I am very happy to have made this journey which has clarified my ideas on various things necessary for my art.' It was the sea, which he was seeing for the first time, which made such a deep impression on him. It seemed to him like a thing, a compact form, a volume 'without a horizon'. Despite these heady discoveries which seem to all young people so personal and exclusive, the umbilical cord tying him to Ornans remained unbroken. In order to understand and express this new and old knowledge, Courbet often studied himself questioningly in the mirror. Durbé has given a most satisfactory explanation of Courbet's so-called narcissism, finding 'the root of Courbet's optimistic vision of the world, of his certainty of his own destiny' in 'his solid moral education in the thrifty comfortably-off world of the country bourgeoisie' whose tenacity stems from 'a historical outlook which puts all its faith in its own daily activity'. And so in the early self-portraits 'we see for the first time Courbet's acute egocentricity, his delight in himself, which was later to become an exaggerated uncontrolled self-admiration, an affirmation of the superiority of his moral world, of his concept of life and reality, of his indisputable talents as the greatest artist of the century: Courbet's so-called narcissism, which both annoyed and charmed his contemporaries, and which, in spite of its notoriety has never been traced back to its source. Far from being a sign of vanity and complacency, or of that morbid desire to make a legend of his own sensibility – common not only to many Romantics, but also to such an apparently reserved and modest man as Millet – this narcissism has very clear social and psychological roots.'

Courbet's *Self-portrait with a Black Dog (pls 3 and 4)* painted in 1842, is a highly refined and yet youthful work. It is steeped in tradition: it has the bitterness of a Giorgione and the technical mastery of a Poussin. But it is also a completely original work. It was with this self-portrait that Courbet made his public debut, exhibiting it at the Salon in 1844 at the age of twenty-five. At about this time he was also developing certain new ideas (also explained by Durbé): the style of painting to be found in the great paintings in the museums is quite suitable for grand subjects. But, for the intimate and tranquil scenes, in the petit-bourgeois taste, Courbet considered that the more mundane style to be found in a particular type of painting current at that time, though not culturally respectable, was more suitable: this was a European kind of Proto-Realism, to be found in Holland, Germany, Scandinavia and Russia, which only today has begun to arouse some slight interest. It is a rough idiom with touches of classical romanticism, and Courbet adopts it in works like *The Hammock (pls 7-8)*. This is a delightful and fascinating painting because it is perilously close to being a provincial, petit-bourgeois, almost *kitsch* version of rococo subjects like ' swings in the garden '. *The Lovers in the Country* (*pl. 6*), also painted in 1844, is a splendid work, but it too has the sugariness of a valentine and is only saved by its sub-title ' Sentiment du jeune âge ' from being totally trivial. Another painting of the same year and of a similar type is the highly successful *Portrait of Juliette Courbet* (*pl. 5*), the artist's youngest sister. It owes its admirable stylistic unity to the sharpness of the disturbingly cold colours, and the drawing which seems to make fun of the girl's slightly quizzical expression and disproportionately large ears.

The painting was refused by the Salon in 1845. Three more paintings were rejected and *The Guitar Player* only managed to scrape in. Dissatisfied but confident as ever, Courbet wrote to his family:

' Small paintings do not bring acclaim. Next year I must paint a large picture which will show me in my true light. I demand all or nothing. Small pictures are not the only thing I can do. I see things on a larger scale.'

It was to be some time before his paintings grew in size but his work did become more substantial, as we can see in his next self-portrait, the famous *Man with a Pipe* (*pl. 9*), his most romantic work and outstanding for its use of colour. At the Salon of 1846, one of his self-portraits, which one we do not know, finally won him favourable criticism from Champfleury, who was to become a friend. His *Portrait of Baudelaire* (*pl. 10*), in the following year, is an indication that his circle of acquaintances was widening. The square genre composition (figure in an interior) in the eighteenth-century manner was undoubtedly a deliberate choice. But the result, which is not entirely successful and which is, even to us, rather strange, pleased neither the artist nor the subject. It almost seems to pre-figure the ambiguous relationship between the two artists with their different approaches to life – Baudelaire's being basically aesthetic, and Courbet's basically moral – which only permitted agreement on the more obvious generalities. Thus Baudelaire, after recognizing that Courbet ' had done much, not only towards re-establishing a taste for simpli-city and candour, but also a selfless, absolute love for painting ' and agreeing to appear in his allegory, *The*

Artist's Studio, later withdrew in disgust from ' that rabble of artists and men of letters, who hide their short-sighted intelligence behind the vague and obscure term, realism '. In 1847 Courbet had the good fortune to meet the dealer van Wisselingh, which gave him the chance to travel to Holland. Courbet's style flourished under the influence of the Dutch masters of the seventeenth and eighteenth centuries. *The Sleeping Girl* (*pl. 12*), painted on his return and finished in 1849, is an outstanding example of his debt to Dutch painting. The work owes much to Rembrandt's poetic use of light, which in turn contributes enormously to Courbet's own handling of volume. The model for the painting was probably Virginie, who bore a son to Courbet in 1847, according to Toussaint. The boy was called Emile Binet, taking the mother's surname, and lived away from his father in Dieppe with his mother's family. He died very young in 1872. Virginie was to leave Courbet a few years after the birth of her son. The failure of this relationship, which was the only stable relationship in Courbet's life, probably led Courbet to seek fulfilment through his vocation as an artist rather than in his personal life.

The February Revolution of 1848 and the declaration of the Second French Republic were important events in the artist's life. The new political situation demanded more from him than the revival of his grandfather's Jacobin ideals or of his father's revolutionary ideals of 1830, with which it seemed to him he had been fighting ' a war of intelligence ' since his arrival in Paris. The moment had come to take the important step of creating a proletarian art. This did not mean making the working classes his subject matter, but creating art for the people, the style and content of which would necessarily be unacceptable to the bourgeoisie, the traditional patrons of art. Clark expresses this aptly when he talks of the creation of a dual public, one to be won over and one which will be antagonistic. Courbet describes his intended public in a letter to his friend Wey in 1850: ' The people have my sympathy. I must turn to them directly, and learn from them and live through them.' Thus not only was he aware that it is for the artist to find the right public, but also, and much more important, he understood that the new culture would arise from values produced by the working class; with these values he would have to imbue his painting.

Theories of Realism were being elaborated in endless and productive discussions among artists and intellectuals in the Brasserie Andler, which opened in 1848 in the Rue Hautefeuille, a few minutes' walk from Courbet's studio and those of his fellow artists. Courbet's main companions were Max Buchon, François Bonvin, Champfleury, Etienne Baudry and Alfred Bruyas (all of whom collected his works), the painter Gigouz and the critic Duranty. The clientele of the Brasserie Andler also included artists like Corot, Daumier, Décamps, Barye, and writers like Baudelaire, Planche, Silvestre, Proudhon and Castagnary. All these men, whose names were inevitably to be linked with Courbet's, were to some extent involved in the formulation and development of Realism. None of then, however, was to become the standard bearer for the theory. It was Courbet, with that hasty, rather reckless arrogance which so often gives rise to crucial choices, who was to take on this task.

We should remember that the 'seven years of artistic life' which led up to the 'true allegory' of *The Artist's Studio* should be counted from 1848. The seven paintings sent to the Salon of 1848 stem from before this period: there is even a classical *Walpurgis Night* in which he pays homage to Goethe. But these seven works are already very close to the goal of Realism. Apart from a portrait and a self-portrait, their theme is the life and landscape of Ornans. Outstanding among them is *After Dinner at Ornans (pl. 11)*. Interpreted perhaps as the homage of a talented and inoffensive young painter, the picture pleased the jury and won Courbet second prize, a gold medal and the purchase of the work by the state. The painting was then placed in the museum in Lille. The prize was to be an embarrassment to later Salon juries, as it was rather awkward for them to repudiate their earlier recognition of Courbet's talents. But Courbet had not cheated: his painting was the size of a historical painting rather than a genre painting, and his revaluation of the healthy and ancient peasant ethos was modern history. It was not Courbet's fault if the jury had seen the subject matter purely as the pretext for a painting, when the subject matter itself was all-important. This is what Ingres meant when he exclaimed in front of the painting: 'How can it be that nature with its own hands spoils its most beautiful works? What wasted values! What sacrificed gifts! . . . This revolutionary will be a disastrous example.'

With this encouragement, Courbet forged ahead. Between 1849 and 1850, he completed some of his best works, which were exhibited first in Besançon then in Dijon, accompanied by an introduction written by Buchon in the socialist magazines of each city, before going to the Salon of 1850-51. The first painting, which no longer exists, was *The Stone Breakers* (see black and white illustration on p. 11). Courbet describes his feelings about the two toilers in a letter to his friends, the Wey family: 'I went to the castle of St Denis to do a landscape: near Maisières I stopped to watch two men splitting stones in the road. It would be hard to come across a picture of greater misery; and so all of a sudden I could see a painting. . . On one side there is an old man of seventy, bent over his work, with raised pick, his limbs tanned by the sun, his head shaded by a straw hat; his trousers made of coarse material are patched, his socks which must once have been blue show his heels. Over there, there is a young man, his head covered in dust, his flesh a greyish colour; his back and arms show through his filthy, tattered shirt, one leather brace holds up the remnants of his trousers, and his muddy leather shoes have many gaping holes. The old man is kneeling, the young man standing behind him is struggling to move a basket full of split stones. Alas! in this sort of work, this is how you start and how you end up. Here and there, their work tools are scattered: a pannier, a shovel, a saucepan, etc. The scene takes place in full sunlight, in the open countryside, along the side of the road. The landscape fills up the picture. Yes. . . we must proletarianize art; for too long, painters of my generation have produced an ideal art, copied from the cartoons. . . '

Art for a new public, that is why it was worth compromis-

The Stone Breakers (see p. 32).

ing art politically. Later in 1865 Proudhon was to explain that Romanticism had been guilty of non-intervention: ' The tacit compromise between Classicism and Romanticism was, like doctrinaire politics, hypocritical. What is killing – and dishonouring – art at the moment, is the confusion and irrationality ... Delacroix expressed his romanticism by revealing his personal impressions; he defined painting as the art of becoming illusion for the spectator and the ideal as everything which suited his personal ideas, thus reducing the reform of art, of which he was the standard bearer, to a simple difference in technique, whereas it was necessary to seek this difference, above all in ideas, in the consciousness of the century, in the state of society.' This is what other leading contemporary painters failed to grasp. They failed because of their lack of culture, because, whether good or mediocre, from Rose Bonheur to Couture, from Chassériau to Meissonier, all of whom were born between 1815 and 1822, they were simply painters. They lacked the sociological insight of Daumier and Millet, and failed to learn from the sociological and political literature

11

of, for example, Balzac, with his dissection of the class differences in French society. The characters in *The Funeral at Ornans* (*pls 15 and 16*), painted by Courbet immediately after *The Stone Breakers* and exhibited with it, belong to the world of the *comédie humaine*, and are addressed to that world. Indeed, Courbet wrote to Champfleury that the whole village was keen to be included in the picture: ' The mayor, who weighs a ton, the curate, the police sergeant, the cross bearer, the lawyer, Marlet, the valuer, my friends, my father, the altar boys, the sexton, two veterans of the 1793 Revolution wearing the clothes of the period, a dog, a corpse and bearers, the church cleaners, one of whom has a nose like a cherry, very large and five inches long, my sisters, other women, etc. have all posed for me already. I thought I could leave out the two parish choristers, but it was not to be. They came to tell me that they were very hurt as they were the only ones in the parish whose portrait I had not painted. They complained bitterly and said they had never done me any harm, and they did not deserve such an insult.'

This local enthusiasm compensated Courbet for the vehement condemnation of the work by the ' antagonistic ' public in Paris which objected to the ' tobacconist's sign style ' (Gautier) and to the contamination by the artist of a legitimate tradition – the Dutch group painting – with a style taken from popular imagery. Champfleury explained: ' Everyone is taken aback by this simple painting, as if it was a naive and crudely made woodcut.' The interest of the figures should not prevent us from looking at the landscape which in this work, as in *The Stone Breakers*, fills the canvas: the sun is setting, with the solemnity of the *De Profundis*, behind the wall of the rocks of Ornans. Proudhon's observations on contemporary painting by Courbet, *Peasants of Flagey returning from the Fair* (*pls 35-36, 37*) (of which today we only have a later replica) could equally well apply to the *Funeral*: ' It is impossible to find any satirical allusions . . . Courbet does not resort to exaggeration, derision or invective; his irony does not degenerate into calumny; he does not become pitiless, nor does he give anyone undue consideration.'

Thus, Courbet painted his large pictures as he had intended, and with them he won renown. Paris was in an uproar. Two of his works went to an exhibition in Brussels (*The Violoncellist* which is a portrait of his friend Alphonse Promayet, who also appears in *After Dinner at Ornans*, painted for the Salon of 1848; and *The Stone Breakers*). Encouraged by this general interest, Courbet found a contemporary subject with great dramatic potential: *The Departure of the Fire-Brigade* (*pl. 17*), a very large work, which Courbet never completed. With this canvas, Courbet aimed to graft contemporary popular themes onto a composition (Rembrandt's *Night Watch*) taken from the history of art. Nochlin (1967) cites the *Sapeur Pompier* which appeared in *L'Illustration* in 1843 and Dupont's *Incendie* as iconographical sources for this work. In the meantime Courbet had lost some of his revolutionary fervour of 1848 and allowed himself a rustic interlude with works like the *Village Girl with Goat* (*pl. 20*) and *The Village Maidens* which was exhibited in 1852 (*pls 21 and 22*). Near their house, Courbet's sisters pose with a young peasant girl and a dog, while over to one side there are two cows drinking. In the Leeds version, which is the better one, the success of the painting derives from the relationship (which is altered in the version in the New York Metropolitan Museum) between the distant landscape marked by a stunted tree, and the tiny figures, whose identity is none the less clearly visible, from the little bunch of brightly coloured rags of the peasant girl, to the circular group of the three sisters. It is possible that on this occasion Courbet tried to see Ornans through the eyes of Corot.

In March, *The Funeral at Ornans* and *The Stone Breakers* were exhibited at Frankfurt-am-Main with great success. Courbet's influence on German art stems from this period and is most noticeable in the work of Leibl and his followers, particularly after 1860. Central and southern Europe (he had already exhibited in Brussels and was to exhibit in Antwerp, Munich and Vienna) were more receptive to a style which drew on seventeenth- and eighteenth-century Dutch Realism and German Proto-Realism.

The end of 1850 marked another political upheaval. Na-

13

poleon III proclaimed the Second Empire. Courbet's close friend Buchon was exiled. He himself remained in Paris, an angry witness to the triumph of the arrogant and philistine bourgeoisie, that *parvenu* society which derived its main pleasures from luxurious and promiscuous living, which moreover it sought to justify. Courbet's reaction was prompt. At the first imperial Salon in 1853 he exhibited three works: *The Wrestlers* (now in the museum in Budapest), *The Sleeping Spinner* (*pls 23-24*) and *The Bathers* at Montpellier (*pl. 19*). The indignation they aroused was such that the Emperor himself actually hit the most shocking of the three works – *The Bathers* – with his riding-crop. Prosper Mérimée commented on the realistic treatment of the human flesh, but said that as, after all, it was not destined to be eaten by cannibals, he saw no good reason for painting it. Even Delacroix was shocked. The painting is certainly a ferocious work: as Proudhon said, the reason the Tartuffes were shocked by the nudity was because it was unconventional, but the work also shows how the peasant's healthy freedom from inhibitions can be corrupted by their aping of bourgeois conventions. The signature in the picture, prominently placed on a large stone, suggests the grin of the ever present voyeur. *The Sleeping Spinner*, on the other hand, and *Women Sifting Grain* which he completed a little later on, in 1854, contain statements of equal weight. With their religious respect for the weariness of labour and the deep tenderness which inspires women's sacrifice, they are the works of Courbet which come nearest to Millet's poetic art, that is, the most idealized of his images designed to serve a social purpose.

He exhibited again in Frankfurt; then, in May, he accepted an invitation to spend the summer with his friend Bruyas, who had been brave enough to buy the two paintings of the previous Salon (*The Bathers* and *The Sleeping Spinner*). We should not be misled by the splendid landscape and marine paintings, which reveal his love for the beach at Palavas, into thinking that this was simply a holiday for Courbet. It was a period of reappraisal, undoubtedly stimulated by the intelligent company of his friend Bruyas. And also at this time, the ideas which were to merge in

The Artist's Studio a year later were becoming clearer. One of the two portraits of Bruyas, which Courbet painted in this period, bears the inscription: 'Study in Modern Art – Solution A. Bruyas' (*pl. 27*). In *The Meeting* (*pls 28-29*), Nochlin (1967) has shown that the artist, painted life-size together with Bruyas and one of Bruyas's servants, intended the work to be an allegory, in which he himself was the Wandering Jew. Courbet's messianic tendencies (Baudelaire once said, 'Here's Courbet come to save the world'), have led him to find the secular and modern equivalent of a *Noli me tangere* in a subject from popular imagery (which was used by Champfleury in an article which appeared some years later, by Eugène Sue in a pamphlet and by Béranger in one of his songs). From Montpellier, before returning to Ornans, Courbet went to Switzerland to visit Buchon. Immediately afterwards he began work on *The Artist's Studio* (*pls 32-34*), which is six metres long and three and a half metres in height, another magnum opus like *The Funeral at Ornans*. In December 1854, while working on this picture, he wrote to Bruyas: 'There are thirty life-size figures. It is the moral and physical account of my studio. They are all the people who help me and take part in my work. I will call it 'first version' because I hope that eventually the whole of society will have passed through my studio and that I shall express all my likes and dislikes. I have two and a half months in which to complete it and I shall even have to go to Paris to do some nudes, so that, all in all, I shall only have two days left for each figure. You will understand that I shall not be amusing myself. Now you should send me my portrait in profile and your portrait, the two that I did at Montpellier and the photograph of a naked woman which I mentioned to you. I shall paint her standing behind my chair in the centre of the painting. Then will come your portrait and the portraits of those artists who have realist ideas.'

He worked at this exhausting pace with the aim of exhibiting the picture at the 1855 Universal Exposition. Universal Exposition – the words must have held an irresistible appeal for Courbet: it was exactly what he wanted for his paint-

15

ing. But he was expecting too much, according to the Minister, Count de Nieuwerkerke: Realism was 'the painting of democrats, people who never change their linen and who have the impudence to impose themselves on decent society.' On behalf of the Government, Nieuwerkerke warned Courbet he could only guarantee to show his work at the exhibition if a sketch of it had been formally submitted to the jury beforehand. Courbet's answer was exemplary, both for its content and as a public expression of the political nature of his indignation (so much so that Cézanne, eleven years later, replied to the same Nieuwerkerke with a letter which was almost identical): if he was sending the paintings, it was because it was in the nature of paintings to be exhibited, and certainly not because he wanted to enter into a competition or be judged by anyone. So it happened that, of the thirteen paintings entered, eleven were accepted and the best two, *The Funeral at Ornans* and *The Artist's Studio* were rejected. But Courbet was not one to take things lying down. With the financial assistance of Bruyas, he set up, in the Rue Montaigne, not far from the Exposition, a pavilion of Realist art which contained an exhibition of forty of his works. In this way he could combine a personal statement with a historical purpose. He had to address 'the moral and physical story of his studio' to the contemporary audience; future generations, on the other hand, would have his manifesto on Realism. His opponents seemed to have won the first victory: had his works been exhibited at the Exposition, they would have had a *succès de scandale*, as at the 1853 Salon; but the public kept away from his own private exhibition. Yet, inevitably, the exhibition was an event of great importance to many: both to the aging Delacroix and to newcomers like Fantin Latour or Whistler, Degas or Pissarro. They saw it as the sign of future victory. With a theoretical clarity which is itself a refutation of his so-called rusticity, Courbet wrote in the catalogue: 'The term "realist" has been applied to me as the term "romantic" was applied to the men of 1830. Labels have never given an adequate description of the things they describe: had they done so, then the works themselves would have been superfluous. Without stopping to discuss the appropriateness of the term, which no-one, I hope, will feel obliged to really understand, I shall confine myself to clarifying the issue, so as to put an end to misunderstandings. I have studied the art of past and modern masters without any programme in mind or any prejudices. I have wanted neither to imitate nor to copy them, nor do I plan to attain the useless goal of art for art's sake. No, I have simply wanted to be able to draw on the whole of our artistic tradition, in order to find a rational and appropriate independent expression of my own individuality.' In conclusion, he wrote: 'To be able to represent the customs, the ideas, the appearance of these times, according to my way of looking at things: to be not only a painter, but a man: in a word, to make living art – that is my aim.' He wrote these few plain-speaking words to those who could understand him. And it was for his moral authority, rather than for his painting in itself, that he gained his reputation as a master with the Impressionists.

Now we come to the 'true allegory', *The Artist's Studio*. Courbet was about thirty-five when he completed it. For his own self-portrait, he used a painting done in the previous year, *Courbet with striped collar*, in which he is less handsome, rather fatter and more affable-looking than in earlier portraits. Immediately afterwards he gave up painting self-portraits with the exception of the self-portrait painted in prison seventeen years later. The figures in the painting represent, on the left, those people who live on the margins of society – the old and the poor, the labourer, the Jew etc., and on the right, his friends, Baudelaire, Bruyas, Buchon, Champfleury, Promayet, Proudhon and other anonymous figures, who stand for all that the artist has learned in the previous seven years in Paris and Ornans. The female model has been taken by some to stand for Truth.

We cannot understand the surprise aroused by the fact that the artist is painting a landscape of Franche Comté with a 'real' sky (Delacroix) rather than a figure painting: we have already tried to show that what Courbet had discovered was the new social aim of art, rather than new subjects. As for the people in his painting, they are not models, they are the 'public': the nude model looking at the canvas is the obvious proof of this.

In the early autumn, after the Realist Pavilion had closed, Courbet went to Belgium to paint landscapes. There he was warmly received. However, in England his work was not to meet with much success. He sent some paintings to an exhibition at the Crystal Palace, London, in 1856. But at that time the Pre-Raphaelite Brotherhood dominated English art, and, even if some people were nearly prepared to die for Realism (such was the case of Millais's model for Ophelia, who posed in water for him), the mystical leanings of the movement were totally opposed to Courbet's achievements, which Rossetti was later to define (in Paris in 1864) as 'filth and rubbish'.

The works completed at the end of 1856 and presented at the Salon of 1857 mark a new period closely related to the problem raised in *The Artist's Studio*. There are fewer figure paintings; in fact Courbet no longer resorted to narrative painting unless an irresistible subject presented itself. He seems to have beeen more attracted by landscape and hunting scenes. *The Quarry* (illustrated in black and white on p. 19) is the first work in this new genre: the painting, which has a splendid colour range, is another allegory. Quite clearly the dead deer to the left and the pool of blood in the centre foreground dominate the work, despite the lively depiction of the spotted coats of the two dogs, the red jacket and shiny instrument of the horn-blower, the ray of light coming from between the tree trunks in the background and the grave and thoughtful figure of the huntsman. If, as I believe, Courbet identifies with this subject, it is with the victim rather than with the remorse of its killer.

The other important painting also exhibited at the Salon of 1857 is the *Young Women on the Banks of the Seine* (*pls 39-40*) once again a painting which shocked the public. Proudhon, who was alone in understanding its meaning (which is a moral one, but a condemnation rather than a sermon), was to write that the painting was the counterpart of *The Stone Breakers* in so far as it portrays the corrupt

The Quarry (see p. 35).

products of urban society. The title, he says, ' is meaningless, one could hardly contrive a worse one. The Seine has nothing to do with it. You can't see it. What the author really wanted to say was: two fashionable young girls during the Second Empire. But a title of this kind would have seemed seditious: it wasn't possible. Note however that the Empire only stands for a date just as the Seine is a metaphor for Parisian society. This is the political content of the picture.' It was enough. The same year saw the publication of Baudelaire's *Les Fleurs du Mal* which seemed to confirm the social ills of Paris under the Second Empire.

Courbet stayed with Bruyas during spring 1858 and spent the following autumn and winter in Germany. He exhibited *Women Sifting Grain* and *The Quarry*. He completed two paintings, the *Lady of Frankfurt (pls 41-42)* and the *Huntsmen's Picnic*, but he also prepared a lot of sketches of hunting scenes at which he was present, which he finished in France. It may be possible to link the mood of romantic uncertainty of these works and their timorousness and psychological instability, evident in the rapid and retouched *Lady of Frankfurt* (the painting is full of second thoughts) with Courbet's passing interest in Menzel. We know that the scholasticism of modern German painting seemed amusing to him, but he was referring to official historical painting. Menzel on the other hand, who managed to resist Courbet's influence for a long time, evidently had an impressive mastery of his own style (which anticipated Naturalism), and this would certainly have interested his fellow painters.

Courbet's stay in Le Havre in the summer of 1859 marked the beginning of the relationship – which was not to mature until several years later – between Courbet and the young Impressionists. Courbet's casual discovery of two paintings by Boudin, which he admired in the window of a frame-maker in Le Havre, and his subsequent meeting with Boudin himself, inspired the latter to write: ' I shall try to make great paintings, important paintings, with a more refined tone. Courbet has a broad conception one could emulate, even if sometimes his work seems rather coarse and unrefined in details.' Boudin's response was typical of the Impressionists' cautious adoption of his poetic imagery. The Festival of Realism which Courbet organized in his studio in the autumn of 1859 marked the beginning of a series of exhibitions in 1860 and 1861: in Paris (Gallerie Martinet), Montpellier, Besançon (Universal Exposition, at which he won a medal), Paris again (Salon), Metz (where he won a medal) and Antwerp. His prestige grew. It was clear to everyone that Courbet would never swerve from his principles. Young people tended to gather round him, because, of everybody, not even Delacroix had been able to help them: elected a member of the jury of the 1859 Salon he had been unable to hold out against Couture, and Manet's painting was rejected. Courbet accepted the young artists' requests to be their teacher and the experiment lasted from January to April, 1862. It should be seen as a gesture of political defiance rather than as the passing on of Courbet's experience to the younger generation. The young artists chose Courbet because he was a master who did not teach; Courbet accepted them because they were pupils who did not learn. It was, on both sides, the most categorical rejection of the concept of an art school. *L'art vivant*, or as Courbet now described it 'historical painting which is essentially contemporary', represented values which every generation had to discover for itself. In the famous 'Letter to his Pupils' he writes: 'Every epoch must have artists who express and represent it for posterity. An epoch which is not able to express itself through its artists has no right to be expressed through artists who come afterwards.'

The thirty or forty artists (among them Fantin-Latour) who went to the studio in Rue Notre-Dame-des-Champs during the four months of the experiment approved of their teacher's gesture and copied the live ox which he gave them as a model. Their aim was to enrage people like Couture. Inevitably, the latter replied in 1865 with a painting called *The Realist*, which shows the painter sitting drunkenly and unsteadily on a classical plaster-cast head, painting a pig's head from life. In early June of the same year, 1862, Courbet went to Saintes at the invitation of his friend Baudry. The ten months he spent there, (discussed by Bonniot in 1969) were a period of intense work which culminated in an exhibition of fifty paintings of landscapes, portraits and still-lifes of flowers and fruit – a new genre for Courbet, to which he was to turn frequently in later life and of which Lemonnier was to say in 1868: 'Courbet knows how to give still-lifes the throb of desirable objects.' During this time, Courbet also developed a disturbing theme for the Salon of 1863, which was, incidentally, also the year of the Salon des Refusés. Courbet's painting was to have the double honour of being refused admittance to both Salons. Writing to a friend from Saintes, he explained: 'I had wanted to know how much liberty was accorded to us these days. I had sent up a painting of priests, *The Return from a Conference*, which meant a great deal to me. This painting was a fitting reply to the Emperor's insult in the previous year, and also accurately described present-day relationships with the clergy. The painting really hit the mark; it hurt where it was meant to hurt. It was taken down and hung up again three or four times. If I had a word with Walewski, I could perhaps get it hung up again for a fifth time. I painted the picture in order for it to be rejected, and I succeeded. And that is my reward. However, as this painting is so terrifying, it would be ridiculous to force the administration's hand.'

The destruction of this painting, by a fanatic, is an important episode in the history of iconoclasm, the most recent one prior to the Nazi crusade against 'degenerate art'. Iconographically the painting is linked with the epic paintings of the road way, *The Stone Breakers (p. 11)*, the *Peasants of Flagey (pls 35-37), The Meeting (pls 28-29)* and later *The Beggar's Alms*. It was Courbet's first venture into the realm of satire, and it brought his work closer in style to that of Goya or Daumier. Proudhon was quick to appreciate the importance of the work, and he offered to present it, together with an essay, for exhibition in England. It was the starting point of his book *Du principe de l'art et de sa destination sociale,* in which Courbet is the protagonist, and which was published posthumously in 1865:

'Imagine, on a main road, at the foot of an ancient, sacred oak, before a sacred image, and beneath the sardonic gaze of a peasant, a scene of drunkards, all belonging to the most respectable of classes – the priesthood ... the seven deadly sins, led by hypocrisy, parade in ecclesiastical costume; the fumes of lust waft among the groups; as a final, striking contrast, this miserable little orgy from

clerical life takes place in a landscape which is both
enchanting and grandiose, as if man in his great dignity
only existed to taint the innocence of nature with his
indelible corruption.'

In that year, 1863, the year of Delacroix's death, the
official Salon bestowed the Legion of Honour on the
academic painter Alexandre Cabanel for his *Birth of Venus*,
and the Salon des Refusés brought glory to Manet for
his *Déjeuner sur l'Herbe*, which owes as much to Courbet's
Young Women on the Banks of the Seine (pls 39-40),
painted seven years earlier, as to a free use of one of
Courbet's sources, Giorgione.

Courbet's work continued to be as controversial as ever.
He dreamed of painting huge murals for railway stations.
He sent *The Awakening* (or *Venus and Psyche*, now lost)
to the Salon of the following year, 1864, thus reacting
to that academically sanctioned pornography, which had
brought such honours to Cabanel, with an equally erotic
painting. We do not need to know whether Courbet was
attacking or going along with public taste, of which
Ingres's *Turkish Bath* was an obvious example. What
distinguishes Courbet's work, however, is that it clearly
describes the perversions of the times; and this was, of
course, quite unacceptable. Only Renoir, that great poet
of eroticism, was fascinated by this new facet of Courbet's art.

In the autumn of 1864, Courbet went first to Salins as
the guest of the Buchon family (*pl. 47*), and then to the
Jolicler family at Pontarlier. In early January the news of
Proudhon's death reached him at Ornans. Courbet immediately replied to the book that Proudhon had dedicated
to his art with a painting dedicated to Proudhon's
philosophy, which he called his 'compass'. He presented
it, still unfinished, at the Salon (*pls 54-56*). As had
happened on other occasions, the painting was admired at
Ornans – where Courbet, working feverishly, completed
it in only thirty-six days – and had a cool reception in
Paris. This was because content weighs more heavily in
the provinces, whereas in the cultural climate of Paris,
more attention is paid to form. Had Proudhon been alive,

23

he himself would have written a fitting literary commentary. Although this is a fundamental work, it is much less allegorical in spirit than many others and less so than might have been expected in this case. The motive force is a memory chosen by the artist as being exemplary, and which he wishes to paint immediately, before it eludes him. The disjointed effects and the inconsistency of perspective from one image to the other stem from the mechanical effort of memory involved in putting together all the pieces of a mosaic as fast as possible. The painting refers back to the year 1853 when Proudhon, whose home was in the Rue de l'Enfer, used to take his things out into the garden so that he could write beside his wife, who worked sitting in an armchair (Courbet remembered her pregnant with their third child), and near the two playing children. It is no accident that the only figure whom the artist is finally forced to eliminate from the painting, *Madame Proudhon, (pl. 57)* is the most real (the friend has disappeared and the children have grown up) and the most out of place. This great picture, as dominating as an image on the cinema screen, whose obsessive fixity repeats forever the imperfection of the irrevocable past, testifies yet again to Courbet's great powers of expression.

During the summer in Trouville, Courbet saw Boudin, Monet and Whistler, whose beautiful companion, Jo, an Irish girl with bright red hair, was the inspiration for several of Courbet's nude paintings. He joined the young people in painting seascapes. Whistler paid him the compliment of painting him, gazing at the sea, as in Courbet's self-portrait at Palavas so many years before. He painted portraits, nudes and fantasies like the fascinating *Girl in a Canoe (pl. 58).*

During this period Courbet often included the motif of a bird (which has sexual overtones) in his paintings of women. The most famous example of this theme is *The Woman with a Parrot (pls 59-60)*. Manet also painted a *Woman with Parrot* in 1866. Whether or not this was intentional, Manet's work is the exact opposite of Courbet's. The subject (the model was Victorine Meurend, who posed nude for the *Déjeuner sur l'Herbe*) only serves to contribute to a formal composition of chromatic values. Courbet's picture has not won general approval. Venturi, for example, called it one of his worst blunders. Certainly the painting can only be accepted or rejected as a whole, according to whether or not you approve of the artist's bold intentions. Preparing the painting for the Salon of 1866, Courbet said: ' If people are not content this year, then they really are difficult to please. I am giving them just what they want, two very suitable paintings, a landscape and an academic study.' Thanks to the Academy, he had a triumphant success.

The thoroughness with which Courbet painted this last cycle of new themes (from now on he was to paint only well-tried themes) meant that they were not without influence on the next generation of artists. *The Woman with the White Stockings*, *The Sleeping Nymph*, *Woman with a Wave*, *The Spring (pl. 73)* and *The Three Bathers (pls 74-75)* are works whose sensuality was to influence Renoir. Lemonnier has aptly described them as ' the transports of a virginal man in a fever of eroticism '. For an enthusiast of the genre, Khalil Bey, the Turkish ambassador, Courbet painted, as a private commission, a work entitled *The Origin of the World*, which really depicted a prostitute having an orgasm. Edmond de Goncourt became an admirer of Courbet through this work with its affinities with Correggio. For the same patron Courbet painted *The Sleepers* (or *Indolence and Sensuality, pls 62-66*). It has as its subject two lesbians, and is a masterpiece of the genre. As the second title suggests, the painting is the closest of his works to Baudelaire. Although the subject is depicted with the most blatant realism, it attains the level of myth, and has the richness and strength of a youthful work.

Courbet was reaching the stage at which Zola complained: ' The admiration of the crowd is always in direct opposition to individual talent. The more you are admired and understood, the more you become ordinary.' At this point, Courbet's life story detaches itself from the history of art, of which the Impressionists now become the protagonists, and becomes simply the difficult and unrewarding life of an artist and a man: at Deauville, in the summer of 1866,

Monet took little heed of the advice of the master and painted one of his first masterpieces, *Women in the Garden*, disregarding the suggestion that he paint a dark background; Cézanne, Pissarro and Guillaumin painted in the style of Courbet, but the Courbet of an earlier period. Courbet felt that the moment had come for a big retrospective exhibition. He was represented by four paintings in the Universal Exposition of 1867, but he exhibited nearly 140 works in a pavilion at the Rond-Point du Pont de l'Alma, to which the public came, tamed, if not yet totally won over. Only the caricaturists made fun of his now undeniable authority. With the foreign admirers came the Tuscan painters, in Paris for the Universal Exposition, who asked Castagnary for a long review for their art journal.

During the last ten years of his life, Courbet returned to old themes. After such a long time, he felt the need to ' paint some new, deeply felt, socialist painting ', like *The Beggar's Alms*, which originates in a subject of 1854 (see Nicholson, 1962). With this work and the *Roebuck on the Alert (pl. 72)* Courbet had his first great confrontation with Impressionism, at the Salon of 1868. The confrontation was repeated at Le Havre during an International Maritime Exhibition, to which (through the influence of Boudin) Courbet, Manet and Monet were invited, and where, together with Boudin himself, all three were awarded prizes. In the same year Courbet exhibited at Gand and Besançon. He sent two works to the Salon of 1869, the *Hallali du Cerf* and the *Siesta*, which the painter Bazille did not think up to Courbet's usual standard, although ' masterpieces in their general flatness '. Their composition, particularly that of the first of these works, is indeed superb. During the summer he went to Etretat on the Channel where he painted some seascapes. *Stormy Sea* and *Cliffs at Etretat (pls 80-81)* are the two masterpieces which he presented at the Salon of 1870. The wave is the symbolic image of unease and passion, as well as having a visual form which is both complete and ephemeral. Courbet depicts it here as a questing image. The rocks, in contrast, are firm and decisive: space, volume, light, shade, air, water, earth are all depicted in the composition with absolute precision.

In the year 1869, among other marks of recognition, Courbet was awarded the gold medal at the Brussels exhibition and the Cross of the Order of St Michael by Ludwig II of Bavaria in Munich. They were cultural honours and Courbet felt able to accept them. In the following year, however, he was to refuse the Legion of Honour, that most official of honours. On his return he spent some time in Interlaken where he painted landscapes (*pl. 78*) before going to Salins to bid farewell to his dying friend, Max Buchon.

The outbreak of the Franco-Prussian War was a crucial event in Courbet's career. He was appointed president of the commission for the protection of works of art threatened by the bombardment, but at the surrender of Paris he left this post to take part in the Commune. His work on the commission did not help him later. The government of the Third Republic, having crushed the Commune, was not looking simply for those responsible for destroying the Vendôme Column (and we do not even know for certain that Courbet was one of them). They really wanted a scapegoat for the many revolutionary cultural ideas elaborated during the Commune (abolition of the Rome Academy, the Ecole des Beaux Arts, the medals awarded at the Salon, etc.). Courbet was sentenced to six months imprisonment. He spent the first few months in the prison of Sainte-Pélagie, and the rest in a hospital in Neuilly. He painted while he was in prison. He had no models, and so he painted still-lifes or repeated old subjects from memory. The most important of his prison paintings is his self-portrait *Courbet in Sainte-Pélagie* (*pls 82-83*). The window is half open, letting in air and the intense light from the courtyard. The traditional puny prison-yard trees, each planted in its little square of earth, almost disappear in the light, whose strength is emphasized by the black rectangles of the cell windows. The window becomes a personal attribute like the black dog or the leather belt, the pipe or the striped collar. But Courbet seems to want to dissociate himself from it, gazing out into the void, and has placed himself in a distorted perspective, which seems to foreshadow the later Cézanne. The design has a restricted, elementary, deliberately rough quality which makes this work a particularly tragic document.

On his release from prison, the works that he sent to the Salon of 1872 were refused for political reasons. Bowed down by the sorrows of these years (between 1870 and 1875 his mother, son, and his sister Zélie died), he took to drink. He was sentenced by a second trial to pay the expenses of reconstructing the Vendôme Column, and his property was confiscated. His desire for peace led to his decision to go and live in Switzerland, where, struggling to re-establish himself and weighed down by the enormous financial burden, he worked with the help of assistants who did the bulk of the paintings which he signed. His health suddenly began to fail. He suffered from cirrhosis of the liver and dropsy, the result of excessive drinking, and was taken very ill in 1877. He died on 31 December. A few days before his death, he was ready to take his leave and pronounced the names of his dear ones for the last time. 'My dear sister, my dear father, do not worry and stay quietly in the warmth, if possible at Flagey.' In 1919, a hundred years after his birth, his remains were taken back to Ornans.

Courbet and the Critics

Courbet made his name as a realist painter. It was Realism which, in the terms of the ambitions of nineteenth-century France, brought him *la gloire*. And since of all the ideologies of the nineteenth century, Realism was the most fiercely defended and opposed, Courbet has been as much the object of myths and prejudice as of dispassionate historical assessment. But of all the one-sided interpretations – and, as is the inevitable fate of such a complex and contradictory figure as Courbet, there have been many – the least justified is the one which ignores the strong ideological and psychological motivations of his work and looks only at the paintings themselves. The image of the revolutionary with paintbrush in hand, or of a bohemian in love with his committed way of life, is preferable. At least this kind of erroneous interpretation gives some idea of the power, if not the quality, of an active form of communication, whose message still reaches its objective – the public.

Mastering the necessary formal and technical means for his painting presented no problem to Courbet and was in fact the least of his problems. He was able to paint well ' from the very first ', as he said himself. It was a gift from nature, as even Ingres reluctantly admitted, though by this he meant an essentially intuitive capacity selectively to assimilate a figurative language, both from the history of art, and from the surrounding landscape, whether it was the natural one or the artificial one of modern life and the early mass media (newspaper illustrations, commercial reproductions, popular songs). Courbet's problem lay in mingling his individual intellectual and sentimental emotions as well as collective experience and aspirations, in an artistic medium which would express them as a universal outlook on life. Of all the portraits from life, drawn by those who knew him (such as Silvestre, Buchon, Champfleury, Castagnary), only Proudhon succeeded in drawing an accurate picture, describing Courbet's genius as ' a great intelligence whose faculties are all concentrated in a single one '. Courbet's powers as a painter made their mark on artists like Picasso and De Chirico, and the many others, both in France and elsewhere, whom we have already shown to have been influenced by him. It is hardly surprising that during the Impressionist period the critics (among whom Lemonnier, D'Ideville and Mantz were the first to analyze Courbet's work after his death) were to concentrate on his work rather than on his personality. This was due less to the emphasis placed on pure painting by the new artists, than to the fact that in comparison with their new and apparently gratuitous audacity, Courbet's work, leaving aside its content (Lemonnier for example defined Courbet as ' a great but stupid painter ') now seemed orthodox and powerful, the work of a classical artist of the French school. Faced from then on with the problem of a choice between form and content, for or against Realism, the critics have taken stands like that of Aragon or Venturi, to give just two examples of opposed methodologies.

Recent, highly specialized studies have succeeded in transcending this alternative and, apart from numerous monographs, some scientific, like Fernier's, or popular, like Boudaille's essay, we shall concentrate on these. We must therefore mention the results of iconographic analyses of the American school (Schapiro, Nochlin) and historical documentary research (Nicholson, Clark) and stylistic research (for example the excellent catalogue for the recent exhibition, compiled by Toussaint, de Forges and Pérot). For a more profound discussion of the place of Courbet and Realism in the history of art, and of aesthetics in the nineteenth century, we must turn to Rewals, Novotny and Durbé. In the light of such contributions, we have a much fuller and less contradictory appreciation of Courbet, based on important facts which can be interpreted in terms of individual psychology and the collective unconscious (of the working class and the petit-bourgeois peasantry) which Courbet expressed from the first, and which was crystallized in Realism. Without Courbet Realism could not have developed in the same way. In fact we can invert the terms used at the beginning of this section and say that Courbet was the glory of Realism.

Notes to the Plates

1 Portrait of Régis Courbet. Private collection, Paris. 73×59.5 cm. Originally belonged to Juliette Courbet, and was put up for sale in 1919. The painting is neither signed nor dated, but certainly dates from no later than 1840 and was painted in Ornans on the eve of Courbet's departure for Paris. The work has been documented since 1906 (Riat).

2 Despair. Private collection. 45×54 cm. It was in the Courbet sale of 1881. Signature and date on the bottom on the left-hand side: 41 G. Courbet. The signature has clearly been corrected. Exhibited for the first time in Vienna in 1873.

3-4 Self-Portrait with a Black Dog. Paris, Musée du Petit Palais. 46×56 cm. Signed and dated on the bottom on the left-hand side: Gustave Courbet 1842. Exhibited for the first time in 1844 at the Salon (the artist's first contribution to a collective exhibition).

5 Portrait of Juliette Courbet. Paris, Musée du Petit Palais. 78×62 cm. Given to the museum by Juliette Courbet in 1909. Signed and dated at the bottom in the centre: Gustave Courbet 1844. Rejected by the Salon of 1845 where it was presented with the title Baroness de M. Exhibited at the artist's first retrospective exhibition in Paris in 1882.

6 The Lovers in the Country. Lyons, Musée des Beaux Arts. 77×60 cm. Initialled and dated at the bottom in the centre: G.C. 1844. Also known by its sub-title *Sentiment du jeune âge* and by the title *Les Amants heureux.*

7-8 The Hammock. Winterthur, Oskar Reinhart collection. 70×97 cm. Signed and dated at the bottom on the left-hand side: 1844 G. Courbet. Recently (see Boudaille 1969) it has been suggested, falsely we believe, that the painting dates from the period of the *Young Women on the Banks of the Seine.*

9 Man with a Pipe. Montpellier, Musée Fabre. Signed at the bottom on the left: G. Courbet. Painted in 1846. With its meditative mood, and the soft and shaded painting, the work is closely related to another self-portrait *The Wounded Man* (see *pls 25 and 26*).

10 Portrait of Baudelaire. Montpellier, Musée Fabre. 53×61 cm. Left by Bruyas to the museum in 1876. Signed at the bottom on the left: G. Courbet. Painted in 1847 or 1848 in Paris in his studio in the Rue de la Harpe; sold in 1859 to Poulet-Malassis from whom Alfred Bruyas bought it in 1874. First mentioned by Champfleury in 1872 (*Souvenirs et portraits de jeunesse*).

11   After Dinner at Ornans. Lille, Musée des Beaux Arts. 195×257 cm. Exhibited at the Salon of 1849, the work won the artist the second gold medal and was bought by the state. The first two figures on the left are Courbet's father and Courbet himself. The violinist is his friend Promayet.

12   The Sleeping Girl. Paris, private collection. 65×53 cm. Neither signed nor dated. Toussaint (1969) has identified the work as *La Dormeuse* of 1849 exhibited at the artist's private exhibition in 1867 in the pavilion at the Rond-Point du Pont de l'Alma. Another painting of the same subject, which belongs to the Institute of Arts in Detroit and is dated 1845, is probably a first step towards *The Sleeping Girl*. The latter shows marked changes in style which stem from the influence of Rembrandt's work, with which Courbet became acquainted during his journey to Holland in 1847. The painting, which was put up for sale in 1881, was bought by Juliette Courbet and has belonged to the De Tastes collection and to Matisse.

13   Valley of the Loue in stormy weather. Strasbourg, Museum. 54×65 cm. Signed twice at the bottom, to the right and left: G. Courbet (the signature on the left is much later). It is not dated and is not mentioned for the first time until very late (Estignard 1897). It has usually been thought to belong to the artist's last period, but recently Toussaint has put its date at 1849 because of the traditional composition in which the foreground is used like wings in a theatre and because the subject corresponds to the title of a landscape exhibited in the Salon of 1849: *Valley of the Loue from the Roche du Mont*. The village on the banks of the Loue is Montgesoye.

14   Grape-picking at Ornans. Winterthur, Oskar Reinhart collection. 53×64 cm. Exhibited at the Salon of 1849 together with six other works including the *Valley of the Loue from the Roche du Mont*, mentioned above, and *After Dinner at Ornans*.

15-16   The Funeral at Ornans. Paris, Louvre. 314×665 cm. Painted in 1849 and mentioned, while he was working on it, in a letter from Courbet to Champfleury.

The Stone Breakers. (Illustrated in black and white on p. 11). Formerly in the Gemäldegalerie, Dresden. 159×169 cm. Signed at the bottom on the left: G. Courbet. Painted in 1849, presented to the Salon in the following year. Destroyed in 1945.

17   The Departure of the Fire-Brigade. Paris, Musée du Petit Palais. 388×580 cm. Painted in 1851, the work is unfinished.

18 Portrait of a Woman. Paris, Roger Hauert collection. 40×32 cm. Signed at the bottom on the right: G. Courbet. Probably dates from around 1850, and may be the same work as the *Portrait of Mademoiselle D.B.* exhibited in 1876 (Toussaint). Mentioned by Riat in 1906 and exhibited at the retrospective exhibition in Besançon in 1952.

19 The Bathers. Montpellier, Musée Fabre. 227×197 cm. Signed and dated at the bottom on the right: G. Courbet 1853. Bought by Alfred Bruyas together with the other painting entered for the Salon of 1853, *The Sleeping Spinner* (see below) and presented by him to the Museum.

20 Village Girl with Goat. Paris, private collection. 80×65 cm. Signed at the bottom on the left-hand side: G. Courbet. Exhibited for the first time at the Pavilion at the Rond-Point du Pont de l'Alma in 1867 with the date 1860. This date is thought by Toussaint to be a printing error, as for stylistic reasons and because Courbet only used this particular model in the years from 1847 to 1853, the painting must date from around 1850.

21-22 The Village Maidens. Leeds, City Art Gallery. 54×66 cm. Signed and dated at the bottom on the left: G. Courbet 51. It was sold by the artist in 1854 and was shown in the following year at the exhibition of his work in the Rue Montaigne. We cannot identify the exact whereabouts of the landscape in the painting.

23-24 The Sleeping Spinner. Montpellier, Musée Fabre. 91×115 cm. Signed and dated at the bottom on the right: G. Courbet 1853. Bequeathed by Bruyas to the Museum. Exhibited at the Salon of 1853 together with *The Wrestlers* (Budapest Museum) and *The Bathers.* This very important painting is dealt with at length by Proudhon who emphasizes that in spite of the realistic but undidactic tone of the work, which is in fact sympathetic and affectionate towards its subject, the public were still extremely hostile towards it.

25-26 The Wounded Man. Paris, Louvre. 81.5×97.5 cm. Signed at the bottom to the left: G. Courbet. Shown at all the artist's personal exhibitions from 1855 onwards. Recent research by de Forges (1969) and X-rays have clarified the history of this painting, of which Courbet was so fond that he did not want to be parted from it. He began the work in 1844 as a composition with two figures like the *Sieste champêtre* and *The Lovers in the Country.* It was entered for the Salon in 1844, 1845, 1846 and 1847 and was always rejected. We do not know what made him dispense with the female figure in the painting or change the rural subject into an autobiographical and symbolic theme: it is possible, however, that Courbet wanted to portray himself alone and wounded after Virginie Binet had left him. He and Virginie Binet are the happy united couple in *The Lovers in the Country* (*pl. 6*). Courbet made one or more copies of this work.

27 Portrait of Alfred Bruyas. Montpellier, Musée Fabre. Signed and dated at the bottom: G. Courbet 54. Painted during Courbet's stay in Montpellier, as the guest of the hotel-keeper Bruyas, who collected his work.

28-29 The Meeting (Good-Morning, Monsieur Courbet). Montpellier, Musée Fabre. 149×155 cm. Signed and dated at the bottom to the left: 54 G. Courbet. First exhibited in 1855.

30 Seashore at Palavas. Montepellier, Musée Fabre. Signed and dated at the bottom: 54, G. Courbet. From the Bruyas bequest. One of Courbet's earliest seascapes. He was to turn to this genre more often in later life. Eleven years later, Whistler, his companion at Trouville, was to dedicate a painting to him with the same composition: the artist deep in thought with the calm sea spread out beind him (*Courbet in Trouville. Harmony in blue and silver*, Boston, Gardner Museum).

31 The Bridge of Ambrussum. Montpellier, Musée Fabre. Dates from 1853-54.

32-34 The Artist's Studio. A True Allegory summarizing a Period of Seven Years in my Life as an Artist. Paris, Louvre. 361×598 cm. Painted in the winter of 1854-55 and described, while he was working on it, in a letter from the artist to his friend Bruyas. Rejected at the Universal Exposition of 1855.

35-37 Peasants of Flagey returning from the Fair. Besançon, Musée des Beaux Arts. 206×275.5 cm. Second version. The original version, shown at the Salon of 1850-51, has disappeared. Although painted rather later and exhibited for the first time at the Pavilion of Realism in 1855, the work belongs to the Ornans 'trilogy' together with *After Dinner at Ornans* and *The Funeral at Ornans*. It is in these works that Courbet elaborates his grandiose fresco of peasant and provincial life, whose unchanging dignity and solemn simplicity he contrasts with the moral and social evils of urban and industrial life (exemplified in *The Stone Breakers* or the *Fleurs du Mal* theme which makes its first appearance in *Young Women on the Banks of the Seine* in 1856).

38-40 Young Women on the Banks of the Seine. 174×200 cm. Signed at the bottom on the left: G. Courbet. He did the sketches at Ornans in 1856 and finished the work in Paris in 1857. Exhibited at the Salon in the same year, it aroused varied reactions. Gautier, for example, believed that Courbet intended the work to shock people, whereas Proudhon thought it moral in intent. But Gautier did recognize the work's pictorial merits, nor did the Impressionists fail to appreciate them. There is a smaller replica of the work (some people believe it to be a preliminary sketch) in the National Gallery in London, and there are also several studies.

The Quarry. (Illustrated in black and white on page 19). Boston, Museum of Fine Arts. 210×180 cm. Signed at the bottom on the right: G. Courbet. Exhibited at the Salon of 1857, the work was already in Boston in 1867 and hence was not shown at the large exhibition at the pavilion at the Rond-Point du Pont de l'Alma. This is one of Courbet's most important works, and is the first on the favourite theme of his mature and later years – the stag hunt.

41-42 Lady of Frankfurt. Cologne, Wallraf-Richartz Museum. 104× 140 cm. Signed at the bottom on the left: G. Courbet. Painted during Courbet's stay in Germany in the winter of 1858-59, it was exhibited for the first time at the pavilion of the Rond-Point du Pont de l'Alma in 1867. It was stolen from a store room and found again in 1873. It was put up for sale in 1919 and belonged to a German collection until it went to the Cologne Museum in 1958. The work has been changed (in the balustrade, the staircase and the little temple in the background, which is painted over the head of a man). Toussaint has pointed out that the painting is exceptional among Courbet's works because of its unreal, suspended atmosphere, which is so unlike the usual solidity of his scenes.

43-44 The German Huntsman. Lons-le-Saunier, Museum. 118× 174 cm. Signed and dated on the bottom at the left-hand side: 59. Gustave Courbet. Exhibited for the first time in Besançon in 1860, sold by the artist to Jean Mazaroz, who gave it to the museum in 1886. Also known as the *Dying Stag*. Sketched in Germany, the work depicts one of Courbet's hunting companions. He finished the painting in France, and used the Levier forest in Franche-Comté for the landscape.

45 Portrait of a Woman with a Parrot. Paris, Alfred Daber collection. 61.5×44 cm. Signed and dated at the bottom on the left: G. Courbet 61. Traditionally regarded as a portrait of Solange Dudevant, the daughter of George Sand, the work only became known after the artist's death. The bird, a parrot with bright plumes, is a motif which often appears in works painted in the 1860s.

46 Portrait of Mademoiselle Gabrielle Borreau. Paris, Alfred Daber collection. 63.5×77 cm. Signed and dated at the bottom on the left-hand side: G. Courbet 62. The work, once thought to be the portrait of Madame Borreau, has now been identified by Bonniot (1969) as the portrait of her daughter. Hence, we know that the painting dates from the artist's stay in Saintes and was exhibited there in 1863. The work, which was well received, shows great technical skill and is influenced by Venetian painting of the Renaissance.

47 Portrait of Madame Buchon. Besançon, Musée des Beaux Arts. 56×46 cm. Signed and dated at the bottom on the left-hand side: Gustave Courbet 1864. Documented from 1897 onwards (Estignard), the work remained in the Buchon family. The 'mother of realism' as Courbet affectionately called her was the very lively wife of Max Buchon.

48 Waterfall at Conches. Besançon, Musée des Beaux Arts. 74×60 cm. Signed and dated at the bottom on the left: Gustave Courbet 1864. Painted during his stay in Salins and sold to a local collector together with a view of the Fort de Joux which is the painting's pendant.

49 Pusset's Farm. Paris, private collection. 54×65 cm. Signed and dated at the bottom on the left: 1864 Gustave Courbet. Painted during his stay in Pontarlier a few miles from the town, just above the village of La Gauffre. Exhibited for the first time at the retrospective exhibition of 1882. This is unusual among his landscapes for the simplicity of the composition which is built on the dark triangle of the fir trees stretching from the background into the foreground.

50 The Reflexion. Douai, Museum. 54×45 cm. Signed at the bottom on the right: G. Courbet. Exhibited at the Rond-Point du Pont de l'Alma dated 1864, and sold by the artist to the city of Douai in 1870. The model appears in many of his paintings of erotic subjects of the period (*Venus and Psyche, The Wave*). The work has a replica which is identical in size and another slightly smaller one.

51 The Stream of the Puits Noir. Toulouse, Musée des Augustins. 80.5×100 cm. Signed at the bottom on the left: G. Courbet. The first owner of the work, Madame Beraldi, gave it to the museum in 1912. Probably painted in 1865 during the period when Courbet spent a long time at Ornans and painted several landscapes of the surrounding countryside, including the Puits Noir, which he also sometimes called the 'covered stream'.

52 The Breme at the junction with the Puits Noir. Besançon, Musée des Beaux Arts. 73.5×92.5 cm. Signed and dated at the bottom on the left: Gustave Courbet 65. Left by Boron to the Museum in 1897.

53 The Clairvoyant. Besançon, Musée des Beaux Arts. 47×39 cm. Signed and dated at the bottom on the left: 65 G. Courbet. Also known as *La Somnambule*. As the work was certainly exhibited in Munich in 1864, we can only assume that Courbet added the date later, with no concern for historical accuracy. Silvestre saw a sketch for the work in Courbet's studio as early as 1856. The painting, which was one of Courbet's favourites, was exhibited at the Universal Exposition of 1867, at Gand in 1868 and in Vienna in 1873. According to Toussaint, the work is probably a portrait of Juliette.

54-56 Proudhon and his Family. Paris, Musée du Petit Palais. 147×198 cm. Signed and dated at the bottom on the left: Gustave Courbet 1865. On a step on the left-hand side is the inscription: P.J.P. 1853. First exhibited at the Salon of 1865. Confiscated by the state in 1873 and sold by auction in 1877, although the artist had intended it to go to the town of Besançon. Bought for the Musée du Petit Palais at the Debrousse sale in 1900.

57 Portrait of Madame Proudhon. Paris, Henneguy collection. 73×59 cm. Neither signed nor dated. Remained in Madame Proudhon's family until 1958, when it was given to the Louvre. Certainly painted in 1865, soon after Proudhon's death, perhaps as a study for the previous work, which was at one time dedicated to the philosopher's entire family. Courbet then decided to remove the figure of Proudhon's wife from the work as she did not fit into the composition.

58 Girl in a Canoe. Paris, Roger Hauer collection. 172×210 cm. Neither signed nor dated. Painted in Trouville in 1865, first mentioned in *Les Salons de W. Burger* (Thóre) in 1870, the painting belonged to Juliette Courbet and, after a sale in 1919, passed into the collection of the famous dealer Ambroise Vollard.

59-60 The Woman with a Parrot. New York, Metropolitan Museum of Art. 129×195 cm. Came to the museum in 1929 from the Havemeyer collection. Signed and dated bottom left: 66 Gustave Courbet. It was a great success at the Salon of 1866.

61 Portrait of a Man. Vevey, Musée Jenish. 194×111 cm. Neither signed nor dated. Found at a second hand dealer's shortly after the artist's death, it came to the museum in 1897. It has always been thought to be a portrait of Max Buchon, Courbet's friend, but Toussaint has questioned this. According to Toussaint the work dates from around 1865. Its chief interest lies in its evident relationship with the work of Manet.

62-66 The Sleepers. Paris, Musée du Petit Palais. 135×200 cm. Signed and dated bottom left: G. Courbet 66. Also known as *Indolence and Sensuality*. Painted in Paris, in the Rue Hautefeuille in the summer of 1866 on his return from Trouville for the collector Khalil-Bey. The latter had a passion for erotic paintings and was very disappointed to have missed the *Venus and Psyche*, which

Courbet had sold shortly before. The red-headed model is Jo, Whistler's mistress, whose portrait Courbet painted several times. The work, which was exhibited for the first time at the retrospective exhibition of 1882, was acquired by the Musée du Petit Palais in 1953.

67 The Covert of the Roe-Deer. Paris, Louvre. Exhibited at the Salon of 1866. Mentioned by D'Ideville in 1878.

68-69 Poachers in the Snow. Private collection. 102 × 122.5 cm. Signed and dated bottom left: Gustave Courbet 67. Painted during the previous winter in Ornans (1866-67) which had been exceptionally snowy. Exhibited at the pavilion at the Rond-Point du Pont de l'Alma in the same year. This is an example of Courbet's famous snow with blue shadows and is a masterpiece of his ' naturalism '.

70-71 Snow Scene with Wild Boar. Paris, Alfred Daber collection. 81 × 100 cm. Signed bottom left: G. Courbet. Landscape of Franche Comté probably painted in winter of 1866-67.

72 Roebuck on the Alert. Paris, Louvre, 66 × 92 cm. Signed bottom right: G. Courbet. Probably dates from 1866 when *The Covert of the Roe-Deer* was shown at the Salon and was so successful that Courbet was showered with commissions for similar paintings. Sold by Courbet to Mazaroz, the painting came to the Louvre in 1926.

73 The Spring. Paris, Louvre. 128 × 79 cm. Signed and dated bottom left: 68 Courbet Gustave. X-rays of the painting reveal a second female figure, which means that we can no longer be sure that this work is the one presented at the Brussels Salon of 1869. It was exhibited and sold in 1882. It was later acquired by Juliette Courbet and subsequently bought by the Louvre at the sale of 1919. It seems likely that this work, together with an analogous composition in the Metropolitan Museum of Art in New York, was Courbet's realist answer to Ingres's academic nudes. The critic Guichard had compared him with Ingres a few years earlier.

74-75 The Three Bathers. Paris, Musée du Petit Palais. 126 × 96 cm. Signed bottom left: G. Courbet. Painted in 1868, it is very close to the previous work. The work inspired Renoir, whose bather seen from behind has obvious links with this painting.

76-77 The Wave (Stormy Sea). Paris, private collection. 66 × 92 cm. Signature bottom left: G. Courbet. This painting, which has recently become well known, is one version of Courbet's famous theme, developed during the summer at Etretat in 1869 and repeated afterwards, even in prison.

78 Landscape at Interlaken. Paris, private collection. 58.5×73.5 cm. Signature and date bottom left: G. Courbet 69. Painted in late summer at Interlaken together with five other landscapes while Courbet was staying there on his return from Munich. It was sold to a Mr Stumpf who had asked Castagnary to let him have one of Courbet's landscapes.

79 Copy of a Self-Portrait by Rembrandt. Besançon, Musée des Beaux Arts. 87×73 cm. Signature and date bottom left: 69 G. Courbet. Confiscated by the state and the given back to Juliette, the work reached the Louvre in 1952 and was given to the Museum in Besançon in 1953. It was painted in the summer of 1869 in Munich, where Courbet was staying while his paintings were being exhibited. In the gallery in Munich he copied a painting by Franz Hals, one by Murillo and one by Rembrandt (today the latter is thought to be an excellent old copy rather than an original Rembrandt). It is interesting that at a time when Courbet had already expressed himself fully in his own artistic language, he should return to the links with the old masters of his formative years.

80-81 Cliffs at Etretat. Paris, Louvre. 130×162 cm. Signature and date bottom left: 70 Gustave Courbet. Exhibited at the Salon of 1870 together with another painting of Etretat, also now in the Louvre: *Stormy Sea.*

82-83 Courbet in Sainte-Pélagie. Ornans, civic collection. 92× 72.5 cm. Neither signed nor dated. Given by Juliette Courbet to the town of Ornans in 1903. First mentioned by Estignard in 1897. This is Courbet's last self-portrait. He had stopped painting self-portraits for the previous fifteen years, but he painted this one in prison as a record of this terrible and historic event.

84 Bowl of Apples. The Hague, Mesdag Museum. 59×73 cm. Signature and date bottom left: G. Courbet 71. Bottom right, inscribed: Ste Pélagie. Exhibited and sold in 1882 to the collector Mesdag. Courbet painted still-lifes in prison, as he was not allowed live models. His first still-lifes of fruit and flowers, most of them out of doors like this one, date from the Saintonge period (1862-63).

85 The Trout. Paris, private collection. 65×99 cm. Signed and dated bottom right: G. Courbet 73. This is another version of the painting in the Zurich Kunsthaus, dated 1871, with the inscription ' in vinculis faciebat '. It seems unlikely that Courbet could have painted this dying trout from memory, and it seems more probable that, like the Paris version and the *Three Trouts of the Loue* in Berne, it too was painted in 1873 in Ornans on the eve of his departure.

86 The Calf. Paris, Mme Léonardo Bénatov collection. 88×116 cm. Signed and dated bottom right: G. Courbet 73. Painted in

Ornans on the eve of his departure into exile. When the peasant who owned the calf knew that Courbet was going to paint it, he carefully washed and combed it. In spite of the refinement of the painting, Courbet was obviously paying homage to Dutch painting, in particular to the Bull by Paulus Potter in the Hague. With Courbet's permission, Cherubino Pata made several copies of the painting.

87-88 The Bridge at Fleurier. Besançon, Musée des Beaux Arts. 65×81.5 cm. Signature and date, bottom left: 73 G. Courbet. It became known in 1951 when it reached the Louvre, which then handed it over the museum in Besançon.

89-90 The Castle of Chillon. Museum, Lons-le-Saunier. 62×69 cm. Signature and date bottom right: G. Courbet 75. Given to the museum by Mazaroz, the work's first owner. This is one of the views of Lake Geneva which Courbet loved to paint while in exile. Many of them were entirely or almost entirely painted by assistants. A list made by Courbet's friend Doctor Blondon, which includes this painting among his authentic works, is of great assistance in sorting out the work of this period.

91 The Goat. Paris, Musée du Petit Palais. 43×33 cm. Signature, dedication and date bottom right: L'Ami Cluseret G. Courbet 76. Given to the museum in 1913 by Théodore Duret. Dedicated to a friend who was also in exile and painted by Courbet in the same year. He painted it from memory. It is a version of the *Dead Goat* in the Mesdag museum, which is in turn a copy of a detail of the large painting in Boston, *The Quarry* (p. 19).

2

3

4

5

6

6

7

21

22

24

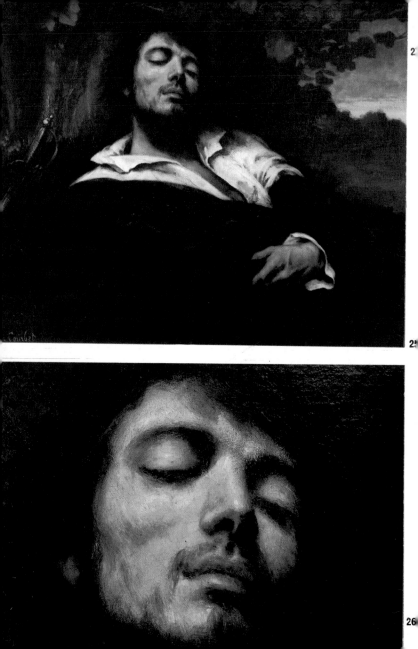

44

45

49

67

68

Gustave Courbet.

84

85